HOCKEY
SUPERSTARS
2012-2013

Your complete guide to the 2012–2013 season,
featuring action photos of
your favorite players

SCHOLASTIC

THE TEAMS

ATLANTIC DIVISION

NEW JERSEY DEVILS

team colors: red, black and white
home arena: Prudential Center
mascot: N.J. Devil
Stanley Cups won: 3

NEW YORK ISLANDERS

nickname: Isles
team colors: orange, blue, white, silver and green
home arena: Nassau Veterans Memorial Coliseum
mascot: Sparky the Dragon
Stanley Cups won: 4

NEW YORK RANGERS

nickname: Blueshirts
team colors: blue, white and red
home arena: Madison Square Garden
Stanley Cups won: 4

PHILADELPHIA FLYERS

team colors: orange, white and black
home arena: Wells Fargo Center
Stanley Cups won: 2

PITTSBURGH PENGUINS

nickname: Pens
team colors: black, gold and white
home arena: CONSOL Energy Center
mascot: Iceburgh
Stanley Cups won: 3

NORTHEAST DIVISION

BOSTON BRUINS

nickname: Bs
team colors: gold, black and white
home arena: TD Garden
mascot: Blades the Bruin
Stanley Cups won: 6

BUFFALO SABRES

team colors: black, white, red, gray and silver
home arena: First Niagara Center
mascot: Sabretooth

MONTREAL CANADIENS

nickname: Habs
team colors: red, blue and white
home arena: Bell Centre
mascot: Youppi
Stanley Cups won: 24

OTTAWA SENATORS

nickname: Sens
team colors: black, red and gold
home arena: Scotiabank Place
mascot: Spartacat
Stanley Cups won: 7 (pre-1934 team)

TORONTO MAPLE LEAFS

nickname: Leafs
team colors: blue and white
home arena: Air Canada Centre
mascot: Carlton the Bear
Stanley Cups won: 11

SOUTHEAST DIVISION

CAROLINA HURRICANES

nickname: Canes
team colors: red, black and white
home arena: RBC Center
mascot: Stormy the Ice Hog
Stanley Cups won: 1

FLORIDA PANTHERS

nickname: Cats
team colors: red, navy blue, yellow and gold
home arena: BankAtlantic Center
mascot: Stanley C. Panther

TAMPA BAY LIGHTNING

nickname: Bolts
team colors: blue, black, silver and white
home arena: St. Pete Times Forum
mascot: ThunderBug
Stanley Cups won: 1

WASHINGTON CAPITALS

nickname: Caps
team colors: blue, black, gold and white
home arena: Verizon Center
mascot: Slapshot

WINNIPEG JETS

team colors: blue, silver, red and white
home arena: MTS Centre

CENTRAL DIVISION

CHICAGO BLACKHAWKS
nickname: Hawks
team colors: red, black and white
home arena: United Center
mascot: Tommy Hawk
Stanley Cups won: 4

COLUMBUS BLUE JACKETS
nickname: Jackets
team colors: blue, red and green
home arena: Nationwide Arena
mascot: Stinger

DETROIT RED WINGS
nickname: Wings
team colors: red and white
home arena: Joe Louis Arena
mascot (unofficial):
Al the octopus
Stanley Cups won: 11

NASHVILLE PREDATORS
nickname: Preds
team colors: navy blue, silver,
white and gold
home arena:
Bridgestone Arena
mascot: Gnash

ST. LOUIS BLUES
team colors: white, navy
blue and gold
home arena: Scottrade Center

NORTHWEST DIVISION

CALGARY FLAMES
team colors: red, gold,
black and white
home arena: Scotiabank Saddledome
mascot: Harvey the Hound
Stanley Cups won: 1

COLORADO AVALANCHE
nickname: Avs
team colors: burgundy, silver,
black and blue
home arena: Pepsi Center
Stanley Cups won: 2

EDMONTON OILERS
team colors: white, navy blue,
orange and red
home arena: Rexall Place
Stanley Cups won: 5

MINNESOTA WILD
team colors:
red, green, gold and wheat
home arena:
Xcel Energy Center

VANCOUVER CANUCKS
team colors: blue, silver,
green and white
home arena: Rogers Arena
mascot: Fin

PACIFIC DIVISION

ANAHEIM DUCKS
team colors: purple, green, silver
and white
home arena: Honda Center
mascot: Wild Wing
Stanley Cups won: 1

DALLAS STARS
team colors: green, white,
black and gold
home arena:
American Airlines Center
Stanley Cups won: 1

LOS ANGELES KINGS
team colors: purple, white,
black and silver
home arena: STAPLES Center
Stanley Cups won: 1

PHOENIX COYOTES
team colors: red, green, sand, sienna
and purple
home arena:
Jobing.com Arena
mascot: Howler

SAN JOSE SHARKS
team colors: teal, gray, orange
and black
home arena: HP Pavilion at San Jose
mascot: S.J. Sharkie

WESTERN

CONFERENCE

YOUR FAVORITE TEAM

Name of your favorite team: _____

Conference and division: _____

Players on your favorite team at the start of the season:

Number	Name	Position
_____	_____	_____
_____	_____	_____
_____	_____	_____
_____	_____	_____
_____	_____	_____
_____	_____	_____
_____	_____	_____
_____	_____	_____
_____	_____	_____
_____	_____	_____
_____	_____	_____
_____	_____	_____

Changes, Trades, New Players

_____   _____   _____
_____   _____   _____
_____   _____   _____
_____   _____   _____
_____   _____   _____
_____   _____   _____
_____   _____   _____
_____   _____   _____

End-of-Season Standings

Fill in the name of the team you think will finish in first place in each of the six NHL Divisions.

EASTERN CONFERENCE

ATLANTIC DIVISION
NORTHEAST DIVISION
SOUTHEAST DIVISION

_____

_____

_____

CENTRAL DIVISION
NORTHWEST DIVISION
PACIFIC DIVISION

WESTERN CONFERENCE

_____

_____

_____

The Playoffs

Which two teams will meet in the Stanley Cup Final? Fill in their names below, then circle the team you think will win.

Eastern Conference Winner: _____

Western Conference Winner: _____

YOUR FAVORITE TEAM

Your Team — All Season Long

The standings of hockey teams are listed on the sports pages of the newspaper all season long. The standings will show you which team is in first place, second place, etc., right down to last place.

Some of the abbreviations you'll become familiar with are: GP for games played; W for wins; L for losses; OT for overtime losses; PTS for points; A for assists; G for goals.

Check the standings on the same day of every month and copy down what they say about your team. By keeping track of your team this way you'll be able to see when it was playing well and when it wasn't.

	GP	W	L	OT	PTS
NOVEMBER 1					
DECEMBER 1					
JANUARY 1					
FEBRUARY 1					
MARCH 1					
APRIL 1					
MAY 1					

Final Standings

At the end of the season print the final record of your team below.

YOUR TEAM	GP	W	L	OT	PTS

Your Favorite Players' Scoring Records

While you're keeping track of your favorite team during the season, you can also follow the progress of your favorite players. Just fill in their point totals on the same day of every month.

player	nov 1	dec 1	jan 1	feb 1	mar 1	apr 1	may 1

Your Favorite Goaltenders' Records

You can keep track of your favorite goaltenders' averages during the season. Just fill in the information below.

GAA is the abbreviation for goals-against average. That's the average number of goals given up by a goaltender during a game over the course of the season.

player	nov 1	dec 1	jan 1	feb 1	mar 1	apr 1	may 1

ZDENO CHARA

Zdeno Chara has an intense off-season, off-ice training routine that helps him start every season a step or two ahead of many of his rivals. Though he'll be 35 years old heading into his 15th NHL season, the NHL's tallest player (he's 6'9") feels that he's in good mental and physical shape. Zdeno may be at an age when many players start thinking about retiring, but he is still thinking about how he can be an even better player.

"I don't think I'll ever be one of those guys who just thinks that 'Okay, this is it. I can't improve anymore.' I like to think that there is always room for improvement, no matter who you are."

"Everything can go right and everything can go wrong in those games. You've just got to make sure everything is almost perfect because that's the game that decides either you play for another day or you're done."
—Chara's thoughts on playing a Game Seven in the playoffs

Zdeno played with the well-known Dukla Trencin junior team in Slovakia for two seasons, from 1994–1996. There, he caught the attention of several NHL scouts. The New York Islanders signed him in the third round of the 1996 NHL Entry Draft. The team urged Zdeno to move to North America for his final season of junior eligibility, which he did. Although he missed 23 games with a broken wrist, he was still the top-scoring defenseman on the Prince George Cougars.

Zdeno spent three seasons with the Islanders, but really started to develop after he was traded to the Ottawa Senators during the off-season in 2001. He also started to show a good offensive touch.

Zdeno was named a First Team All-Star in 2004 and was the runner-up for the Norris Trophy as the best defenseman in the NHL. He played one more season with the Sens before signing as a free agent with Boston. It is with the Bruins that he has become one of the best defenders — and leaders — in the game. Zdeno won the Norris Trophy as the league's best defenseman in 2009 and was an important part of the Bruins' blueline when the club won the Stanley Cup in 2011.

Zdeno still has another five years to go in his deal with the Bruins, and he's showing no signs of slowing down.

DID YOU KNOW?
Zdeno is the tallest player ever to play in the NHL. In bare feet he is 6'9" — on skates he is just under seven feet tall.

HOCKEY MEMORIES
After winning the Stanley Cup in 2011, Zdeno took it to the main square in his hometown. He says that the welcome he received from the fans, close friends and family is one of his greatest hockey memories.

GP	G	A	PTS	PIM
79	12	40	52	86

New York Islanders' 3rd choice, 56th overall, in 1996 NHL Entry Draft
1st NHL Team, Season: New York Islanders, 1997–1998
Born: March 18, 1977, in Trečín, Czechoslovakia (now Slovakia)
Position: Defense
Shoots: Left
Height: 2.06 m (6'9")
Weight: 116 kg (255 lbs.)

MARIAN GABORIK

Last season was a year of improvement and turnarounds for the New York Rangers. As a team, their defensive play improved, and they made it all the way to the Stanley Cup semi-final before falling to New Jersey. They ended the season with 109 points — their highest since they won the Cup in 1993–1994. And Marian Gaborik made his own turnaround, bouncing back from a disappointing 2010–2011 season: he led the Rangers in scoring with 41 goals and 35 assists for 76 points. It was the third-highest points total of his career and his best season since 2009–2010 when he posted a career-best 86 points.

"I came into [last] season determined to come back from the season before and show people that I could still score and be an important player," says Marian.

Most Rangers fans had expected that Marian would get a helping hand when veteran Brad Richards was signed in the off-season. It made sense: Richards' playmaking skills would work nicely with Marian's touch around the net. It did happen, but it took a while for the Gaborik-Richards combination to come together. Coach John Tortorella put the two on a line at the start of the season, but then broke them up. He tried again later in the season. This time they clicked.

"I try to go out there and do my best every night. From a hockey point of view, I hope I'm exciting to watch."

"I think it took the both of us some time to get to know one another on the ice a little better," says Marian. "You get to know when you're using a give-and-go, when to move, what the other guy is doing. It makes a big difference."

Marian hit the career 300-goal mark last season and will probably hit 700 career points if has another solid season this year. Though he'll turn 31, he hopes he has many good seasons still in front of him.

"I'm feeling good right now," says Marian. "I don't feel like 30. It just feels like a couple of years ago that I started playing."

DID YOU KNOW?
Marian was the first draft pick in the history of the Minnesota Wild franchise. When he left the team after eight seasons, he was the last original member of the franchise in the lineup.

HOCKEY MEMORIES
There are few bigger thrills for a player than the Stanley Cup playoffs. In Marian's first playoff year with Minnesota, he led the team on a playoff run with 9 goals and 8 assists in 18 games as the Wild went to the Conference Championship.

2011–2012 STATS

GP	G	A	PTS	PIM
82	41	35	76	34

Minnesota Wild's 1st choice, 3rd overall, in 2000 NHL Entry Draft
1st NHL Team, Season: Minnesota Wild, 2000–2001
Born: February 14, 1982, in Trečín, Czechoslovakia (now Slovakia)
Position: Right Wing
Shoots: Left
Height: 1.85 m (6'1")
Weight: 93 kg (204 lbs.)

MARIAN HOSSA

It's a relatively short list: Players who have scored 900 points in the NHL. Thousands have played in the NHL over the years, but fewer than 100 (96 as of the start of this season) have achieved 900 points. The most recent player to do so was Chicago veteran Marian Hossa. He joined the 900-point club on March 20, 2012, in a game against the Columbus Blue Jackets. It was a typical goal for the veteran: moving in toward the goal from the middle of the slot on the power play, he took a great pass and quickly snapped it into a wide-open net.

That 900th point was part of a very satisfying season for Marian. For a start, he managed to stay healthy. He played in 81 games last season, the most games he had played since 2006–2007, when he played all 82 games with Atlanta. He also finished last season with 29 goals and 48 assists for 77 points to lead his team in scoring — the first time since 2006–2007.

"I had a goal heading into the season that I wanted to play in 80 to 82 games," says Marian. "It just felt really good to be able to play in that many games and contribute and not be fighting injuries."

Marian's game has changed since his first season in 1997–1998, when he was focussed on scoring. However, his game has changed since then. Although he'll never be called a highly defensive player, Marian can now get excited about playing well in both ends of the rink.

"I learned a lot watching guys like Pavel Datsyuk in Detroit," says Marian, recalling one of the best defensive players in the world and a former teammate. "Scoring goals or passing for an assist is fun, but so is the other part of the game."

"I'm not a superstar, no. A star, well, maybe."

Marian signed a 12-year deal with the Blackhawks in 2009. So chances are pretty good that he'll be in a Chicago sweater when he achieves his next career milestone: 1000 points.

DID YOU KNOW?

Marian cuts three different sticks to three different lengths before every game. This way each stick flexes differently.

HOCKEY MEMORIES

Some of Marian's earliest hockey memories are of staying up late in his native country of Slovakia to watch Wayne Gretzky play in the Stanley Cup playoffs. Gretzky remains one of Marian's hockey heroes.

JIMMY HOWARD

Jimmy Howard loves the pressure that comes with being the number one goalie on one of the most successful teams in the NHL. Like the rest of his teammates, the expectations don't seem to worry him at all.

"There is a calmness in our room; we don't get rattled at all," says Jimmy. You look at a guy like Nick Lidstrom, and see how relaxed he is, and how can you not be? That's what our team is like."

Jimmy is heading into his fourth full season with the Red Wings. He has clearly established himself as one of the best in the league. He came out of USA Hockey's National Team Development Program, which provides some of the best coaching and competition for some of the best young players in the United States. Jimmy then went on to an excellent three-year career at the University of Maine, where he was named the team's Most Valuable Player in his final season. He spent most of the next four seasons improving his game with the Red Wings' minor league team. When he arrived at Detroit's training camp in 2009, he was ready to make the step to the big team. In his rookie season with the club, Jimmy grabbed the number-one spot. He played in 63 games and, at one point, started 25 straight games. He became only the fourth goalie in franchise history to win 30 or more games in his rookie season. Jimmy has continued to improve, and both he and the team have high hopes for the future.

"It just goes to show if you have a dream and you set goals and you want to accomplish something, you can."

Jimmy is an important part of a great team. General manager Ken Holland and his staff have put together an organization that many teams envy. They are coming off their NHL-record twelfth consecutive 100-plus point season. Detroit has won more games since 1997–1998 than any other team in the league. With that success comes pressure. But Jimmy wouldn't have it any other way.

"I love the pressure that's put on us," he says. "Every single year it's: 'Stanley Cup or bust,' and expectations are high. It should be that way. It's Detroit."

DID YOU KNOW?
Jimmy holds the unfortunate distinction of being the first NHL goalie to face a penalty shot in each of his first two games in the NHL.

HOCKEY MEMORIES
After Detroit's 2008 championship, Jimmy spent his day with the Cup hosting a backyard Stanley Cup party for friends and family at his parents' place in Ogdensburg, New York.

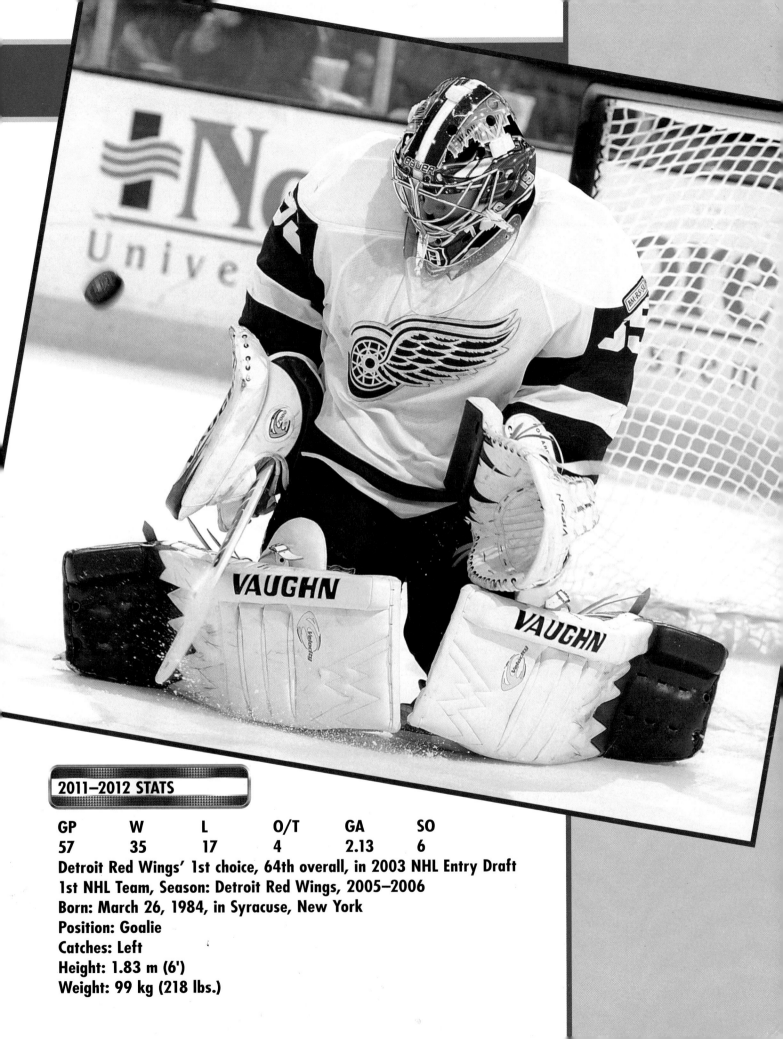

2011–2012 STATS

GP	W	L	O/T	GA	SO
57	35	17	4	2.13	6

Detroit Red Wings' 1st choice, 64th overall, in 2003 NHL Entry Draft

1st NHL Team, Season: Detroit Red Wings, 2005–2006

Born: March 26, 1984, in Syracuse, New York

Position: Goalie

Catches: Left

Height: 1.83 m (6')

Weight: 99 kg (218 lbs.)

JAROME IGINLA

Can there be any doubt that Jarome Iginla is the finest player ever to wear a Calgary Flames sweater? He's still an active player and he's already the all-time franchise leader in games played, goals and points. He has led the team in goals in 10 of the last 11 seasons.

Jarome's latest milestone came on January 7, 2012. It was there, in front of a sell-out crowd, that he scored his 500th career goal as the fans chanted, "Iggy, Iggy!" Jarome became only the 42nd 500-goal scorer in NHL history and the first player in Flames' history to hit that mark.

"I've been very blessed in hockey to have some great moments and memories that will stick with me," says Jarome, "but that's one that I'll definitely remember. It's definitely a lot more special to do it at home and as part of a win."

As great as that moment was, it was one of only a few bright spots in another tough season for the Flames — a season when they missed the playoffs for the third time in a row.

"You're angry, disappointed — disappointed in yourself," said Jarome after it was made official that the Flames would once again miss the playoffs. "We had an opportunity and we didn't make the most of it. We can only look at ourselves and know that we didn't get it done."

"I'd love to play for a lot longer. I feel good and everything, but you know, it goes fast.

The question many Flames fans are asking themselves is whether or not a man who has played every game of his NHL career with the team will be traded now that his greatest years are behind him. But Jarome has a no-trade clause in his contract that he would have to waive before he could be traded. He loves the city, his teammates and playing for the Flames, yet he knows that everything is assessed after a losing season.

"It's part of the game. It's what should happen. We all have to deal with it."

Spoken like a true captain and a great player.

DID YOU KNOW?
Jarome's full legal name is Jarome Arthur Leigh Adekunle Tig Junior Elvis Iginla.

HOCKEY MEMORIES
One of Jarome's greatest memories is also a highlight for Canadian hockey fans: he slid a beautiful pass onto Sidney Crosby's stick, and Sid scored the gold medal-winning overtime goal for Canada at the 2010 Vancouver Olympics.

2011–2012 STATS

GP	G	A	PTS	PIM
82	32	35	67	43

Dallas Stars' 1st choice, 11th overall, in 1995 NHL Entry Draft
1st NHL Team, Season: Calgary Flames, 1996–1997
Born: July 1, 1977, in Edmonton, Alberta
Position: Right Wing
Shoots: Right
Height: 1.85 m (6'1")
Weight: 94 kg (207 lbs.)

EVANDER KANE

Evander Kane is big, strong and heading into his fourth NHL season at just 21 years old. Evander is coming off his best season yet, finishing up as the Jets' second-leading scorer with 30 goals. His totals in goals, assists and points have all increased since his rookie season.

Evander describes himself as "a goal scorer . . . that's what I do best."

With that in mind, it wouldn't be a surprise to see his totals go up again this season.

"He's a very good young player and he's still learning," says Jets' head coach Claude Noel.

Evander was a highly hyped junior player with the Vancouver Giants in the Western Hockey League. NHL scouts at the time identified him as "a guy who played bigger than his size" and who could "surprise a lot of opponents with his strength going to the net."

Evander was selected as the fourth overall pick by the Atlanta Thrashers in the 2009 draft. He stepped right into the NHL as a 19-year old. He did well, finishing seventh among rookies in goal scoring with 14 goals. His strong performance as a young player wasn't a big surprise to anyone who had watched him develop in junior hockey. Evander had played in the Memorial Cup with Vancouver when he was only 15 years old. He had also helped Canada to a gold medal at the 2009 World Junior Championship.

> "I don't really try to be like any special player. I just try to go out there and play the way I play."

Perhaps one of the biggest changes that Evander has had to make has been off the ice, moving from a non-hockey market in Atlanta to a hockey city in Winnipeg.

"It's been an adjustment," says Evander. "It's a lot different. In a hockey country like Canada, all eyes are on you. It's fun."

Jets fans are hoping things get a little more fun this year for Kane and the Jets. A playoff spot would be a good start.

DID YOU KNOW?

Evander's dad was a professional boxer when he was younger and named his son after one of the greatest heavyweights of all time: Evander Holyfield.

HOCKEY MEMORIES

Evander was cut from Canada's 2009 World Junior Championship team but got a second chance when he was brought in as a replacement for a player who was injured. The team went on to win the gold medal, with Evander contributing 6 points in 6 games.

GP	G	A	PTS	PIM
74	30	27	57	53

Atlanta Thrashers' 1st choice, 4th overall, in 2009 NHL Entry Draft
1st NHL Team, Season: Atlanta Thrashers, 2009–2010
Born: August 2, 1991, in Vancouver, British Columbia
Position: Left Wing
Shoots: Left
Height: 1.88 m (6'2")
Weight: 88 kg (195 lbs.)

ERIK KARLSSON

Erik Karlsson's hockey career is already pretty amazing for a player heading into only his fourth year in the NHL. Six seasons ago he had to sit out a season back home in Sweden. Now he has over 200 NHL games under his belt, and last season, won the Norris Trophy as the league's best defenseman. He's also played for Sweden's national team at both the junior and senior level.

"When you look at him, you can see he has all the talent in the world," says teammate Sergei Gonchar. "He can skate, he can shoot the puck. He can stickhandle. He has a bright future."

Erik has made good decisions in his young career and has done things his way as much as possible. For example, the season he sat out back home was partly because he wanted to move to a better organization (Frölunda Göteborg) that he felt would help his development more than the team he was with. Another good decision was to play another season at home in Sweden after he was drafted by Ottawa. Many young European players make the mistake of immediately heading over to North America, only to end up playing in the minors. Not Erik.

"I'm not going to sign with an NHL club until I'm mature enough to play there," said Erik in 2008. "It's better to play here [Sweden] than in the American Hockey League."

"I'm a puck-moving defenseman. I'll do everything I can to shoot the puck and pass the puck fast. That's what I'm good at."

Erik's game took a big step forward last season. Over just one season, his plus-minus went from a −30 to a +16. That means that he was on the ice more often when the Senators scored than when they were scored against — an important statistic for a defenseman.

Erik's impressive offense was one thing. It was, in many ways, expected. He was drafted because of his offensive ability. But it's the combination of offense and defense that will make him a big part of the Ottawa Senators' championship hopes for many years to come.

DID YOU KNOW?

Last season. Erik came very close to recording the highest points total for any Swedish-born defenseman in NHL history. His total of 78 just missed the mark of 80 points set by Detroit's Nicklas Lidstrom in 2005-2006.

HOCKEY MEMORIES

Erik was in awe when he showed up at his first NHL All-Star Game in 2011 and was surrounded by some of the best players in the world. "You are a bit nervous. You don't really know how to act, what to do or say at first."

2011–2012 STATS

GP	G	A	PTS	PIM
81	19	59	78	42

Ottawa Senators' 1st choice, 15th overall, in 2008 NHL Entry Draft

1st NHL Team, Season: Ottawa Senators, 2009–2010

Born: May 31, 1990, in Landsbro, Sweden

Position: Defense

Shoots: Right

Height: 1.83 m (6')

Weight: 82 kg (180 lbs.)

EVGENI MALKIN

When Pittsburgh superstar Sidney Crosby had another on-again, off-again season as he continued to struggle with concussion-like symptoms, the Pens needed their other offensive leaders to step up. Evgeni Malkin was the one to do it, and in a big way. "Geno" put together an outstanding season, leading the team and winning his second NHL scoring title with 109 points. He was also named the Hart Trophy winner as the NHL's Most Valuable Player. Although Evgeni had had big offensive seasons in the past, last season was perhaps a little unexpected. Evgeni was coming off of an injury to his right knee that ended his 2010–2011 season.

That injury came on February 4, 2011, against the Buffalo Sabres when he went heavily into the boards. He was barely able to put any weight on his right leg as he made his way off the ice. Knee surgery followed, but there were concerns about how quickly he would be back on skates. Fortunately for the Pens, Evgeni was in the lineup to start the season and looked like his old self. He really stepped it up in early December, after it was clear that Crosby would be out for quite a while. As if to put his teammates' minds at ease, Evgeni scored 30 points in the next 18 games. During that stretch, Evgeni either scored or assisted on 30 of the 53 goals the team scored.

> **"I try to play 100 percent every game, but a line is three guys playing well."**

"Watching him play at that level without Sidney in the lineup and really carry our team offensively has been pretty impressive," said coach Dan Bylsma. "He's been dominant on the ice. He's been good at both ends of the rink, and he's been the best player, the most dominant player, in the league."

"I think everyone plays a little harder with Sid out," said Evgeni. "You just don't think about the injuries. You go out and play our system. We know how to play."

Evgeni made it through the season injury-free and Crosby made it back into the lineup — so, with fingers crossed, Pittsburgh fans are dreaming of a big year with both their superstars in good health.

DID YOU KNOW?

In 2008–2009 Evgeni became the first NHL player since 1992 to win both the NHL scoring title and the Conn Smythe Trophy as the playoff MVP in the same year. The player who won in 1991–1992? Pittsburgh legend Mario Lemieux.

HOCKEY MEMORIES

You never forget your first NHL goal. Evgeni's was in his first NHL game, on October 18, 2006, against New Jersey. In fact, he went on to score a goal in each of his first 6 games.

GP	G	A	PTS	PIM
75	50	59	109	70

Pittsburgh Penguins' 1st choice, 2nd overall, in 2004 NHL Entry Draft
1st NHL Team, Season: Pittsburgh Penguins, 2006–2007
Born: July 31, 1986, in Magnitogorsk, USSR (now Russia)
Position: Center
Shoots: Left
Height: 1.90 m (6'3")
Weight: 88 kg (195 lbs.)

EDMONTON OILERS

When you come into the NHL as the first overall pick, you can't just start your career quietly. People always expect a lot from you. In his rookie season with the Oilers, Ryan Nugent-Hopkins lived up to those expectations. The things people hoped to see in his game — quickness, anticipation and a good shot — were all there. His future is a bright one.

"There's a little bit of [Joe] Sakic in him . . . he has the puck, you think he's passing, and he shoots. He's got that great release," says Edmonton head scout Stu MacGregor.

Although he missed 20 games due to injuries, Ryan still ended up tied for first place in rookie scoring with 18 goals, 34 assists for 52 points. Even more impressive was the fact that he played on one of the weaker teams in the NHL (the Oilers had the second-lowest points total in the league).

The good news for Ryan and the Oilers is that the future looks bright. The team has an excellent group of talented young players, and Ryan is an important member of that group.

"It was a good experience for me," Ryan said at the end of the season. "I learned a lot this year and got lucky coming to a team like this with such a big group of young guys, and older guys really helping to lead us."

You don't have the kind of success that Ryan has had without having a great work ethic — and you can expect that he'll work hard in the off-season to continue to improve.

"We made some steps in the right direction. Our specialty teams were good and we had some stretches where we were really good."

"I want to get stronger and make sure I get faster and get my shot better," says Ryan. "And faceoffs will be important for me, too."

The Oilers have a lot of work to do, and turning things around doesn't always happen quickly. But Ryan is part of one of the most exciting young teams in the NHL and a franchise that has a tradition of success. So maybe it won't be too long a wait for the Oilers and their fans.

DID YOU KNOW?

As a 16-year-old, Ryan had 65 points in 67 games as a rookie in the Western Hockey League with Red Deer and was named the WHL Rookie of the Year.

HOCKEY MEMORIES

One of Ryan's great hockey memories is of going to the world famous Quebec International Pee-wee Hockey Tournament in Quebec City. It was his first experience playing so far from home and in a big tournament.

GP	G	A	PTS	PIM
62	18	34	52	16

Edmonton Oilers' 1st choice, 1st overall, in 2011 NHL Entry Draft

1st NHL Team, Season: Edmonton Oilers, 2011–2012

Born: April 12, 1993, in Burnaby, British Columbia

Position: Center

Shoots: Left

Height: 1.85 m (6'1")

Weight: 79 kg (175 lbs.)

TOMAS PLEKANEC

Last season was a season of unrest and disappointment in Montreal. It was the worst start to a season for a Montreal team in 70 years. The coach was fired and then, later, the general manager.

"Our job as players is to get ready for what is next," said Tomas Plekanec, who has been in the Habs system since 2001. "It's been tough for the whole season. It wasn't a good year for the players. We need to get ready for next year and prevent those things from happening again."

Even with all the changes in Montreal, Tomas managed a solid season, finishing with the second-highest assist total (35) on the club and ending up fourth in team scoring with 52 points. Still, he is well aware of the expectations and pressure that will be on this year's team not to repeat last season.

"Montreal is like an experience you don't get anywhere else in the world," says Tomas. "People love their hockey. I love to play; I love the rink full of 21,000 fans every game."

Many of those fans have come to appreciate Tomas's work ethic.

With the exception of last season, he has been one of Montreal's best two-way players the last few years. On many nights, Tomas won't focus as much on scoring but rather on trying to shut down the other team's best center.

Simple things, like hard work and mental preparation for the game, are very important to Tomas.

"When I was younger, I was always the first guy on the ice. You have to know what you want to do, know how to get prepared."

"I would say 70 to 80 percent of your performance is mental. All the players can skate; they can play, they can shoot, pass — but it's 'are you ready mentally and how do you get prepared?'" Tomas says.

This will be a pressure-filled season for the Canadiens — but the betting is that Tomas will be well prepared.

DID YOU KNOW?
Tomas is an excellent inline hockey player and has, on several occasions, represented the Czech Republic in international tournaments.

HOCKEY MEMORIES
Tomas' first NHL game was at home on December 31, 2003, against Dallas. He was proud to have his parents there to watch him as he realized one of his life's dreams.

2011–2012 STATS

GP	G	A	PTS	PIM
81	17	35	52	56

Montreal Canadiens' 4th choice, 71st overall, in 2001 NHL Entry Draft
1st NHL Team, Season: Montreal Canadiens, 2003–2004
Born: October 31, 1982, in Kladno, Czechoslovakia (now Czech Republic)
Position: Center
Shoots: Left
Height: 1.80 m (5'11")
Weight: 90 kg (198 lbs.)

JONATHAN QUICK

LOS ANGELES KINGS

The Los Angeles Kings haven't been blessed with any great goalies. But Jonathan Quick is sure to go down as one of the greatest in Kings' history. Last season he helped lead the team to its first Stanley Cup Championship and was also named the winner of the Conn Smythe Trophy as the playoffs' Most Valuable Player.

Early last season Jonathan became the youngest goalie, and only the third in franchise history, to record 100 wins. He also broke Rogie Vachon's 1975 record for the longest consecutive shut-out streak. And amazingly, the Kings had a goalie that received consideration for the Vezina Trophy as the top netminder in the NHL.

"He's a competitor. He has the right mental make up for a goalie," says Kings' Vice-President and Assistant General Manager Ron Hextall, who was a former Philadelphia Flyers goalie.

Jonathan comes from Hamden, Connecticut, an area that has a proud hockey tradition, and he grew up as a fan of the New York Rangers.

Jonathan played a couple of seasons at the University of Massachusetts before spending a full season, and part of the next, in the minors. He arrived to stay with the Kings in December of 2008.

"Everybody's compete and battle level goes up a little bit. It's a harder game. It's a more physical game. Every play matters."
—Jonathan talks about the playoffs

"It's a big adjustment coming up from the minors," recalls Jonathan. "Everything happens quicker. You have less time to make decisions, so your decisions have to be better ones. But at the same time your teammates and the coaching staff around you is also better, so you get a lot of help from that."

Jonathan knows that success in the playoffs is how many goalies and teams are judged by their fans. The last couple of seasons have been good ones for the Kings' young netminder — and his play in last season's playoffs was excellent.

"That's what you work for, all summer, all year."

Heading into this season, it's a confident goalie and a confident team in Los Angeles.

DID YOU KNOW?
Jonathan was the third goalie on the US Olympic Team in 2010 in Vancouver. He practised with the team, but never dressed for a game. However, as a member of the team, he still received a silver medal.

HOCKEY MEMORIES
Some of Jonathan's earliest hockey memories are of playing street hockey with his friends back in Hamden, Connecticut. He can't remember a time he wasn't the goalie.

2011–2012 STATS

GP	W	L	O/T	GA	SO
69	35	21	13	1.95	10

Los Angeles Kings' 4th choice, 72nd overall, in 2005 NHL Entry Draft
1st NHL Team, Season: Los Angeles Kings, 2007–2008
Born: January 21, 1986, in Milford, Connecticut
Position: Goalie
Catches: Left
Height: 1.85 m (6'1")
Weight: 96 kg (212 lbs.)

TYLER SEGUIN

It's tough to call Boston superstar forward Tyler Seguin a surprise so far in his NHL career. He was, after all, a second overall draft pick. Those players are expected to do well. But did anyone really expect him to be the team's offensive leader in only his second NHL season? Probably not. Certainly not Boston fans, who last year voted him the winner of the team's "Seventh Player Award." The award is voted on by the fans and goes to the player who "performed beyond expectations."

"I feel very humbled and honored about accepting this award," says Tyler. "There are a lot of guys who could have got it and it feels really good to have been picked by the fans."

Tyler had a fairly ordinary rookie season in 2010–2011. He played in 74 games and managed 11 goals and 11 assists. Nothing wrong with that, but it wasn't exactly a sign that he was going to come out with a team-leading 29 goals and 38 assists for 67 points the following season.

"I had a few personal goals heading into the season, and I thought I had pretty much kept most of them," said Tyler. "Obviously you want to keep improving . . . I think there is always room for improvement."

Tyler was drafted out of the Ontario Hockey League, where he played for the Plymouth Whalers. He was a center in junior hockey, but has played mostly right wing in his two NHL seasons. Bruins' coach Claude Julien is impressed that a player so young has been so adaptable.

"I see the game better now than I used to . . . I've learned some little tricks out there that have helped me."

"He gives us a lot of options," says Julien. "If we need him at center, we know he can play there. But who knows where he's going to play? We do know that, wherever we do play him, he'll be able to handle it. He'll be strong."

DID YOU KNOW?

When Tyler scored 2 goals and 2 assists in the second period of game two of the 2011 Conference Final against Tampa Bay, he tied an NHL record for most points in one period in a playoff game.

HOCKEY MEMORIES

Winning the Stanley Cup in his rookie season is number one, but a close second was winning the Conference Championship and knowing that the Bruins would have a shot at the Cup.

ANAHEIM DUCKS

Last season was full of milestones for one of the greatest players of his era: Anaheim Ducks right-winger Teemu Selanne.

Teemu's career started in 1992–1993. As a 22-year-old rookie, he scored an amazing 76 goals and 132 points with the Winnipeg Jets — an NHL rookie record that still stands. In 1995–1996, Teemu was traded by the Jets to the Mighty Ducks of Anaheim, where his successful career continued. Meanwhile, the Winnipeg franchise was sold and moved to Phoenix at the end of that season. Zoom ahead to the 2011–2012 season: once again Winnipeg had an NHL team and Teemu was getting ready to play his first NHL game in the city since the trade.

"I still remember the phone call telling me I was traded," recalled Teemu before last season's return to Winnipeg with the Ducks on December 17, 2011. "When I got traded I never really got the chance to say goodbye to the people and the city."

The chants of "Teemu" and the ovations started even before the puck drop, as Winnipeg fans finally had a chance to say thanks to one of the biggest sports stars in the city's

history. It was an emotional night for the "Finnish Flash."

Then, on March 12, 2012, Teemu had another special night as he scored a goal against the Colorado Avalanche and became the highest-scoring Finnish-born player in NHL history with 1,399 career points. He broke the record of his boyhood hero, the great Jari Kurri. Two nights later it was another milestone for Teemu as he recorded his 1,400th career point, becoming only the third European-born player, and 19th player in NHL history, to reach that plateau.

> "I couldn't be more proud that Teemu is the all-time NHL top scorer from Finland. Congratulations to a great player, a great friend and an even better person."
> —Finnish hockey legend Jari Kurri

Teemu finished his 19th NHL season, at the age of 41, with 26 goals, 40 assists for 66 points to lead the Ducks in scoring.

"I still feel great most nights," says Teemu. "When I was 25 I had the same feelings. So, obviously, that's a good sign."

DID YOU KNOW?

Before he became an NHL superstar, Teemu was a kindergarten teacher in Finland for three years.

HOCKEY MEMORIES

Teemu is one of the greatest Olympic hockey players ever. He has played in five Olympic Games for Finland and has scored more points than any other player from any country in Olympic competition (20 goals, 17 assists for 37 points).

2011–2012 STATS

GP	G	A	PTS	PIM
82	26	40	66	50

Winnipeg Jets' 1st choice, 10th overall, in 1988 NHL Entry Draft
1st NHL Team, Season: Winnipeg Jets, 1992–1993
Born: July 3, 1970, in Helsinki, Finland
Position: Right Wing
Shoots: Right
Height: 1.83 m (6')
Weight: 89 kg (196 lbs.)

Last season, Steven Stamkos once again displayed a goal-scoring touch that is second to none in the NHL. Steven lit it up with a league-leading 60 goals. He is only the 20th player in NHL history to score 60 goals in a season. The last player to do that was Alex Ovechkin in 2007–2008.

"It hasn't really hit me yet," said Steven after he'd scored number 60.

The goal came in the last game of the season for the Lightning, 3:29 into the final period of their game against the Winnipeg Jets. He zipped a wrist shot past Jets' goalie Ondrej Pavelec from the left slot. For Steven, it brought back memories of 2009–2010, when he also scored a milestone goal on the final day of the season. That year it was his 51st, which ended up tying him with Sidney Crosby for the NHL goal-scoring title.

"Yeah, it's kind of funny how it came down to the wire both times, but I was fortunate enough to have it all work," says Steven.

Steven was already keeping some pretty good company before he notched his 60th. Earlier in the season, when he scored his 50th, he became only the sixth player in NHL history to have scored 50 goals in a season twice before reaching the age of 23. A couple of the other names on that list are all-time greats Wayne Gretzky and Mario Lemieux. No player in the NHL has scored more goals than Stamkos in the last three seasons.

> *"What I like is that he just pushes always for more. He just wants more all the time . . . it's not just the goals. He never has enough of getting better."*
> —Tampa Bay coach Guy Boucher

Like any good team player, as happy as Steven was with his personal success, he felt his accomplishment was a little bittersweet because the team struggled and fell short of making the playoffs.

"Not making the playoffs outweighs anything you do personally," says Steven. "It's a team game and we've got to get back there."

DID YOU KNOW?

Steven likes to collect hockey sticks. He has a few of his own (including his first NHL goal stick), but also sticks from fellow NHLers Vincent Lecavalier and Evgeni Malkin.

HOCKEY MEMORIES

Steven describes the Tampa Bay playoff run of 2011, when they lost in the Eastern Conference Championship series, as the most fun he's ever had playing hockey.

2011–2012 STATS

GP	G	A	PTS	PIM
82	60	37	97	66

Tampa Bay Lightning's 1st choice, 1st overall, in 2008 NHL Entry Draft
1st NHL Team, Season: Tampa Bay Lightning, 2008–2009
Born: February 7, 1990, in Markham, Ontario
Position: Center
Shoots: Right
Height: 1.85 m (6'1")
Weight: 85 kg (188 lbs.)

Many people in the hockey community argue about whether or not the NHL has a "concussion problem." Some feel more players are suffering from concussions than they did 10 or 15 years ago. But one can't argue the fact that some of the game's brightest stars were on the sidelines for long periods last season, suffering from concussions. Sidney Crosby, Daniel Sedin and Chicago captain Jonathan Toews are three examples of players fans didn't get a chance to watch play for a full season because of their injuries. Jonathan missed 22 games and, like all players suffering from this type of injury, had to be careful about how quickly he returned to the lineup.

"I didn't expect any of this," said Jonathan during his recovery last season. "I had a concussion two years ago, and after two weeks, I felt like myself again and hopped right back in. The toughest thing then was getting the legs back, but that was it. It was history. I didn't look back at all."

Jonathan is one of the most exciting young players in the game. He was a huge part of the rebirth of one of the NHL's oldest franchises, helping to bring the Blackhawks a Stanley Cup Championship in 2010. To go along with the Stanley Cup, Jonathan was also named the Conn Smythe Trophy winner as the Most Valuable Player in the playoffs. As much as Jonathan appreciated it at the time, knowing how tough it is to get back there makes him even more appreciative of how special an accomplishment that championship was.

"I can't imagine any better situation to start out my career in the NHL than these years that I've spent in Chicago. It's been unbelievable."

"You realize the year after how special the team you had was," says Jonathan. "I think the moment all those things are happening, you don't realize how unique and how special it is."

Hawks fans believe that, with their young captain healthy, they're right back on track to win another championship.

DID YOU KNOW?

When Jonathan was named the 34th captain of the Chicago Blackhawks on July 17, 2008, he was the third-youngest player in NHL history to be named a team captain.

HOCKEY MEMORIES

Jonathan will always remember 2010: he won an Olympic gold medal in his home country, a Stanley Cup championship and, to top it all off, was named the Conn Smythe Trophy winner as the Most Valuable Player in the playoffs.

Last season was a season of turnarounds for the Florida Panthers. In one season they went from a team that finished in last place in the Eastern Conference, to a team that finished in first place in their division and had the seventh-best record in the conference. They won eight more games than the season before, scored more goals and gave up fewer. This all led to the club's first playoff appearance in 10 seasons.

Kris Versteeg was a big part of this change for the Panthers. He was brought in as part of a deal with the Philadelphia Flyers. He joined several new faces in the lineup, including forward Tomas Fleischmann and goalie José Théodore. There was also a new head coach, Kevin Dineen. With all of those changes, many experts picked the Panthers to finish last in the conference again. That kind of talk didn't sit well with Kris.

"It's something you take with a grain of salt, but at the same time you get mad at those things," said Kris late last season. "You don't really want to prove people wrong, but you more want to go out and prove yourself right; prove that we have a pretty darn good team. Our success didn't surprise us at all."

Kris did his part by putting together the best season of his career. He finished with a career high 23 goals and 54 points. He also chipped in with eight power-play goals, the second-best total on the team.

"Here, I almost feel like I'm home. It just feels comfortable right away."

One guy not surprised by Kris's big year was Florida general manager Dale Tallon, who had traded for Kris once before, when he was general manager in Chicago.

"I knew when I brought him here what kind of a player he would be," says Tallon. "He's versatile enough to play any forward position and brings passion and commitment to the rink every single day."

Kris has his name on the Stanley Cup already (with Chicago in 2010), and he's determined to get it on there again with the Panthers.

DID YOU KNOW?

Just in case he has to jog his memory, Kris has a tattoo on his right arm to remind him of the date the Hawks won it all: 06-09-10.

HOCKEY MEMORIES

Kris's rookie season was pretty special. He led all rookies in assists and was second in points. He was also named a finalist for the Calder Trophy.

GP	G	A	PTS	PIM
71	23	31	54	49

Boston Bruins' 4th choice, 134th overall, in 2004 NHL Entry Draft
1st NHL Team, Season: Chicago Blackhawks, 2007–2008
Born: May 13, 1986, in Lethbridge, Alberta
Position: Right Wing
Shoots: Right
Height: 1.80 m (5'11")
Weight: 83 kg (183 lbs.)

REFEREE SIGNALS

Do you know what is happening when the referee stops play and makes a penalty call? If you don't, then you're missing an important part of the game. The referee can call different penalties that result in anything from playing a man short for two minutes to having a player kicked out of the game.

Here are some of the most common referee signals. Now you'll know what penalties are being called against your team.

Boarding
Checking an opponent into the boards in a violent way.

Charging
Checking an opponent in a violent way as a result of skating or charging at him.

Cross-checking
Striking an opponent with the stick, while both hands are on the stick and both arms are extended.

Elbowing
Checking an opponent with an elbow.

High-sticking
Striking an opponent with the stick, which is held above shoulder height.

Holding
Holding back an opponent with the hands or arms.

Hooking
Using the blade of the stick to hold back an opponent.

Icing
Shooting the puck across the opposing team's goal line from one's own side of the rink. Called only if the opposing player touches the puck first.

Interference
Holding back an opponent who does not have the puck in play.

Kneeing
Using a knee to hold back an opponent.

Misconduct
A ten-minute penalty — the longest type called. Usually for abuse of an official.

Roughing
Shoving or striking an opponent.

REFEREE SIGNALS

Slashing
Using the stick to strike an opponent.

Spearing
Poking an opponent with the blade of the stick.

Slow whistle
The official waits to blow his whistle because of a delayed offside or delayed penalty call. Done while the opposing team has control of the puck.

Tripping
Tripping an opponent with the stick, a hand or a foot.

Unsportsmanlike conduct
Showing poor sportsmanship toward an opponent. For example: biting, pulling hair, etc.

Wash-out
Goal not allowed.

FINAL TEAM STANDINGS 2011-2012

EASTERN CONFERENCE

Atlantic Division

Team	GP	W	L	OT	PTS
NY RANGERS	82	51	24	7	109
PITTSBURGH	82	51	25	6	108
PHILADELPHIA	82	47	26	9	103
NEW JERSEY	82	48	28	6	102
NY ISLANDERS	82	34	37	11	79

Northeast Division

Team	GP	W	L	OT	PTS
BOSTON	82	49	29	4	102
OTTAWA	82	41	31	10	92
BUFFALO	82	39	32	11	89
TORONTO	82	35	37	10	80
MONTREAL	82	31	35	16	78

Southeast Division

Team	GP	W	L	OT	PTS
FLORIDA	82	38	26	18	94
WASHINGTON	82	42	32	8	92
TAMPA BAY	82	38	36	8	84
WINNIPEG	82	37	35	10	84
CAROLINA	82	33	33	16	82

WESTERN CONFERENCE

Central Division

Team	GP	W	L	OT	PTS
ST. LOUIS	82	49	22	11	109
NASHVILLE	82	48	26	8	104
DETROIT	82	48	28	6	102
CHICAGO	82	45	26	11	101
COLUMBUS	82	29	46	7	65

Northwest Division

Team	GP	W	L	OT	PTS
VANCOUVER	82	51	22	9	111
CALGARY	82	37	29	16	90
COLORADO	82	41	35	6	88
MINNESOTA	82	35	36	11	81
EDMONTON	82	32	40	10	74

Pacific Division

Team	GP	W	L	OT	PTS
PHOENIX	82	42	27	13	97
SAN JOSE	82	43	29	10	96
LOS ANGELES	82	40	27	15	95
DALLAS	82	42	35	5	89
ANAHEIM	82	34	36	12	80

GP = Games played; W = Wins; L = Losses; OT = Overtime; PTS = Points

Top Ten Points Leaders 2011-2012

PLAYER	TEAM	GP	G	A	P	S	S%
1 EVGENI MALKIN	PITTSBURGH	75	50	59	109	339	14.7
2 STEVEN STAMKOS	TAMPA BAY	82	60	37	97	303	19.8
3 CLAUDE GIROUX	PHILADELPHIA	77	28	65	93	242	11.6
4 JASON SPEZZA	OTTAWA	80	34	50	84	232	14.7
5 ILYA KOVALCHUK	NEW JERSEY	77	37	46	83	310	11.9
6 PHIL KESSEL	TORONTO	82	37	45	82	295	12.5
7 JAMES NEAL	PITTSBURGH	80	40	41	81	329	12.2
8 JOHN TAVARES	NY ISLANDERS	82	31	50	81	286	10.8
9 HENRIK SEDIN	VANCOUVER	82	14	67	81	113	12.4
10 PATRIK ELIAS	NEW JERSEY	81	26	52	78	164	15.9

GP = Games played; G = Goals; A = Assists; P = Points;
S = Shots; S% = Percentage

Top Ten Goalies — Total Wins 2011-2012

PLAYER	TEAM	GP	W	L	OT	SA%	GA	GAA
1 PEKKA RINNE	NASHVILLE	73	43	18	8	.923	166	2.39
2 MARC-ANDRE FLEURY	PITTSBURGH	67	42	17	4	.913	153	2.36
3 HENRIK LUNDQVIST	NY RANGERS	62	39	18	5	.930	123	1.97
4 MIKE SMITH	PHOENIX	67	38	18	10	.930	144	2.21
5 JONATHAN QUICK	LOS ANGELES	69	35	21	13	.929	133	1.95
6 JIMMY HOWARD	DETROIT	57	35	17	4	.920	119	2.13
7 MIIKKA KIPRUSOFF	CALGARY	70	35	22	11	.921	162	2.35
8 TIM THOMAS	BOSTON	59	35	19	1	.920	132	2.36
9 ANTTI NIEMI	SAN JOSE	68	34	22	9	.915	159	2.42
10 ILYA BRYZGALOV	PHILADELPHIA	59	33	16	7	.909	141	2.48

GP = Games played; W = Wins; L = Losses; OT = Overtime and/or Shut-Out Losses;
SA% = Save percentage; GA = Goals Against; GAA = Goals-Against Average

END-OF-SEASON STATS

Countdown to the Cup 2012–2013

EASTERN CONFERENCE

**CUP
FINAL**

**CONFERENCE
FINAL**

**CONFERENCE
SEMI-FINALS**

THE CHAMPION:

**CONFERENCE
QUARTER-FINALS**

WESTERN CONFERENCE

CONFERENCE FINAL

CONFERENCE SEMI-FINALS

CONFERENCE QUARTER-FINALS

NHL AWARDS

Here are some of the major NHL awards for individual players. Fill in your selection for each award and then fill in the name of the actual winner of the trophy.

HART MEMORIAL TROPHY

Awarded to the player judged to be the most valuable to his team. Selected by the Professional Hockey Writers Association.

2012 winner: **Evgeni Malkin**

Your choice for 2013: _____

The winner: _____

ART ROSS TROPHY

Awarded to the player who leads the league in scoring points at the end of the regular season.

2012 winner: **Evgeni Malkin**

Your choice for 2013: _____

The winner: _____

CALDER MEMORIAL TROPHY

Awarded to the player selected as the most proficient in his first year of competition in the NHL. Selected by the Professional Hockey Writers Association.

2012 winner: **Gabriel Landeskog**

Your choice for 2013: _____

The winner: _____

JAMES NORRIS TROPHY

Awarded to the defense player who demonstrates throughout his season the greatest all-round ability. Selected by the Professional Hockey Writers Association.

2012 winner: **Erik Karlsson**

Your choice for 2013: _____

The winner: _____

VEZINA TROPHY

Awarded to the goalkeeper judged to be the best. Selected by the NHL general managers.

2012 winner: **Henrik Lundquist**

Your choice for 2013: _____

The winner: _____

MAURICE RICHARD TROPHY
Awarded to the player who scores the highest number of regular-season goals.

2012 winner: **Steven Stamkos**

Your choice for 2013: _____

The winner: _____

WILLIAM M. JENNINGS TROPHY
Awarded to the goalkeeper(s) who played a minimum of 25 games for the team with the fewest goals scored against it.

2012 winners: **Brian Elliott and Jaroslav Halak**

Your choice for 2013: _____

The winner: _____

LADY BYNG MEMORIAL TROPHY
Awarded to the player judged to have exhibited the best sportsmanship combined with a high standard of playing ability. Selected by the Professional Hockey Writers Association.

2012 winner: **Brian Campbell**

Your choice for 2013: _____

The winner: _____

FRANK J. SELKE TROPHY
Awarded to the forward who best excels in the defensive aspects of the game. Selected by the Professional Hockey Writers Association.

2012 winner: **Patrice Bergeron**

Your choice for 2013: _____

The winner: _____

CONN SMYTHE TROPHY
Awarded to the player most valuable to his team in the Stanley Cup Playoffs. Selected by the Professional Hockey Writers Association.

2012 winner: **Jonathan Quick**

Your choice for 2013: _____

The winner: _____

BILL MASTERTON MEMORIAL TROPHY
Awarded to the player who best exemplifies the qualitites of perseverance, sportsmanship and dedication to hockey. Selected by the Professional Hockey Writers Association.

2012 winner: **Max Pacioretty**

Your choice for 2013: _____

The winner: _____

AUTHOR'S ACKNOWLEDGEMENTS: Thanks to NHL.com,
NHLPA.com, the Hockey Hall of Fame, and the personal websites of
players profiled as well as IIHF.com, hockeydb.com and eliteprospects.com
for additional sources of information.

Illustrations by Bill Dickson

Photo credits:
Chara, Kessel: Graig Abel/NHLI via Getty Images
Gaborik: Gregg Forwerck/NHLI via Getty Images
Hossa, Howard: Bill Smith/NHLI via Getty Images
Iginla: Mike Ridewood/Getty Images
Kane: Bruce Bennett/Getty Images
Karlsson: Norm Hall/NHLI via Getty Images
Malkin: Gregory Shamus/NHLI via Getty Images
Nugent-Hopkins: Jeff Vinnick/NHLI via Getty Images
Plekanec: Francois Lacasse/NHLI via Getty Images
Quick: Harry How/Getty Images
Seguin: Jim McIsaac/Getty Images
Selanne: Noah Graham/NHLI via Getty Images
Stamkos: Len Redkoles/NHLI via Getty Images
Toews: Andy Devlin/NHLI via Getty Images
Versteeg: Steve Babineau/NHLI via Getty Images

ISBN 978-1-4431-1971-9 (U.S. Edition)
ISBN 978-1-4431-1901-6 (Canadian Edition)
Copyright ©2012 by Scholastic Canada Ltd.
All rights reserved.

6 5 4 3 2 1   Printed in Canada 118   12 13 14 15 16

FSC
MIX
Paper from
responsible sources
FSC® C011825
www.fsc.org